2ND GRADE HISTORY:
THE MAYAN CIVILIZATION

Speedy Publishing LLC
40 E. Main St. #1156
Newark, DE 19711
www.speedypublishing.com

The Maya civilization was a
Mesoamerican civilization
developed by the Maya peoples.

The Ancient Mayan lived in the Yucatán around 2000 B.C. This area is southern Mexico, Guatemala, northern Belize and western Honduras.

The Maya civilization is famous for its architecture. Many pyramids, temples, palaces and observatories are still standing today.

The Maya writing system was made up of 800 glyphs. Some of the glyphs were pictures and others represented sounds.

The Maya
considered crossed
eyes, flat foreheads,
and big noses to be
beautiful features.
In some areas they
would use makeup
to try and make their
noses appear large.

The Ancient Maya developed the science of astronomy, calendar systems and hieroglyphic writing.

The Maya are perhaps most famous for their work in stone. Maya ceramics are an important art form.

Sometimes the ball games that the Maya played were part of a religious ceremony. The losers were sacrificed to the gods.

9 798886 945162